AF270917

365 SOCIAL MEDIA
POST IDEAS
FOR MASSIVE BUSINESS ENGAGEMENT

A YEAR OF SOCIAL CONTENT PROMPTS
TO GROW YOUR
FOLLOWERS, FANS AND FORTUNE

SARAH CORDINER

A GIFT FOR MY READERS

Get Sarah's **'Course Creation Starter Kit'**

for FREE and learn how to turn your knowledge and expertise, into a highly profitable online course, coaching program or membership academy

Simply visit: www.sarahcordiner.com/starterkit
Join the Facebook group
'Entrepreneur to Edupreneur'

....

CONTENTS

WE ARE HUMAN
PEOPLE IN THIS
DIGITAL WORLD

Do you remember when Facebook first started, and the 'publish a post' prompt from Facebook was

"[Your name] is: ……………………..……………………………"?

So, when I logged onto Facebook, my 'publish an update' prompt said

"Sarah Cordiner is:…………………..……………………………".

This meant that in the early days of Facebook, engagement was created by people simply sharing what they were doing, thinking or feeling in that moment.

This allowed people to peek into each other's lives; to see inside each other's realities that were usually hidden.

We began to get to know each other on a different level; deeper than we ever had before.

We got to get intimately close to people, without leaving our bedrooms.

And so it began.

The free speech, the sharing of ourselves, the exposure of our lives - and, a whole new world of connections, friendships and opportunities.

By encouraging us to share who we are, share our lives, goals, dreams, pains and opinions - Facebook created an empire that makes billions of dollars a day.

And it all comes from our inherent human need for connection, acknowledgment and belonging.

Before we get started with our content, let me ask you this…

Do you have connections online, that you would consider 'friends', but haven't met 'IRL' [in real life]?

If you answered yes, then HOW did you connect with these people?

WHY did you connect?

WHAT is it that took you from complete unknown strangers, to digital friends and allies?

It is likely because both of you discovered that you have something in common.

However, there is a bit more to the psychology and sociology of how your online friendships have formed and it is important that we consider these BEFORE we start creating our social media content.

Why?

Because the people who we are going to be sharing our content with are humans too; and the most successful businesses remember that people are people - not faceless, walking ATM cash machines that empty upon seeing a random social media post.

If we focus on *building friendships* with our prospects, our businesses will flourish.

So how do we build friendships?

What is it that takes two people from strangers, to acquaintances, to friends, to BFFs?

Understanding this, and then creating our content with this in mind, will dramatically improve the effectiveness of your social media content strategy AND the reputation and income that it generates for your business.

THE INGREDIENTS OF FRIENDSHIP

INTERACTION

First we need to cross paths. We need to come into contact with each other more than once.

This means that the more regularly your post, then more opportunities people have to digitally 'bump into you' and begin an interaction.

SOMETHING IN COMMON

The difference between a casual passing, and an interaction that will continue to another interaction, is the discovery of something in common. The same kind of work, the same life goals, the same beliefs, the same frustrations, the same family structure, the same age, the same kind of clothes and so on.

It is important in your posts that you share who you are, what you care about and what you believe in - if you want to create connection, engagement, fans, followers and friends.

SELF-DISCLOSURE

Self-disclosure usually illustrates the moment that people move from 'familiarity' to 'friendship'. As the breadth and depth of what people share gets wider, the deeper the friendship is moving.

As people take the risks of disclosing private and personal information with each other, the friendship grows in trust, strength and longevity.

If your social media posts and content are self-disclosing (in a way that compliments your brand), and encourages your followers to share personal information about themselves too - your connections will deepen and trust will build.

EMOTIONAL INTIMACY

Finally, friendships move into 'BFF' status when an emotional intimacy begins. This is when reciprocity develops, when the level of intimate self-disclosure becomes equal, and when there is an intuitive responsiveness between the pair that always makes the other feel as though they are cared about and valued. It's when the response they get feels like just what they needed in that moment - that they are understood, seen, acknowledged and that the other person just 'gets' them at a soul level. They feel 'seen' even when what they wanted to be seen wasn't openly expressed.

When we engage, respond and love our followers as human beings, as friends, we develop a deep level of trust, dependability and mutually-boosting self-esteem that makes the other want to listen and act for the other almost without restriction.

See your fans as friends, treat them like friends - and your reputation, brand and bottom line (as well as your happiness), will grow beyond your wildest dreams.

The more your share of yourself, the more frequently you do it, the more your engage - the bigger your following and business will grow.

As we now move into the prompts - please keep these points in mind as you draft your content.

BE BUSINESS-MINDED

Yes, we are here to make friends, to build relationships and to build a fan-base of followers who love us.

BUT, we must remember that this is also still a business, and we need these adoring fans to take action - preferably, to buy something.

I strongly recommend that with every post you share, you also include a call to action of some kind.

This could be to get a freebie from you (that they must give you their email address to access), one of your paid offers, the link to your calendar to book a call with you or even the link to an affiliate product that you'll get commission from if somebody buys.

You're here to make fiends, but you're also here to make money.

So do not forget that call to action on every post.

TELL STORIES

I don't mean 'once upon a time' fairy-tale stories.

I mean, SHOW people inside your life and experiences with descriptions, emotion and energy.

Always tie the story back to your audience - relate it to something they can connect with or learn from.

These prompts are merely to give you a starting point of inspiration.

If you want the best results, take each prompt as the starting point to tell a story.

For example, one of the prompts is simply 'Throwback Thursday'.

Although posting an old throwback photo is content, you'll get the most responses, connection and engagement if you used that prompt to tell a story about that time, how you were feeling, what happened to you, what you did, what the 'moral of the story' was and how that metaphorically or directly relates to a lesson for your audience.

I have left space for you on each prompt page to make notes, jot down ideas, determine your call to action and plan your hashtags.

And, if you really want to take this challenge to the next level, the come and join my '#30Days30Tips Challenge' where we push each other to grow our social media engagement, followers, fans and leads together: www.sarahcordiner.com/30days

Ready to make friends AND money?

Let's go!

To your success x

 JANUARY

1st January

Use the theme of 'new beginnings' today.
Remind people who you are and
how you got started.
Share your 'origin story', what the 'backstory'
is to you ending up in your line of work.

Notes, Ideas, Metaphors, Story

....
....
....

Related lesson for my audience

....
....
....

Call to action & Hashtags

....
....
....

2nd January

Post a sneak peek of something coming soon.
Get people excited.
Better yet, get them INVOLVED.
Get them to pick a colour, name it,
choose something about it.
The more involved people become in
the development of something, the
more they want to see the result.

Notes, Ideas, Metaphors, Story

....
....
....

Related lesson for my audience

....
....
....

Call to action & Hashtags

....
....
....

3rd January

Post a testimonial from a client.
This could be a photo, screen shot, a
video or even a live interview.

Notes, Ideas, Metaphors, Story

....
....
....

Related lesson for my audience

....
....
....

Call to action & Hashtags

....
....
....

4th January

Post a bucket list of #22ThingsToDoin2022 and ask your followers to give theirs in comments

Notes, Ideas, Metaphors, Story

....

....

....

Related lesson for my audience

....

....

....

Call to action & Hashtags

....

....

....

5th January

Post a cool morning ritual to start your day.

Notes, Ideas, Metaphors, Story

....
....
....

Related lesson for my audience

....
....
....

Call to action & Hashtags

....
....
....

6th January

#MotivationMonday: share a motivational quote, story, or video and use the #MotivationMonday hashtag in your update

Notes, Ideas, Metaphors, Story

....
....
....

Related lesson for my audience

....
....
....

Call to action & Hashtags

....
....
....

7th January

#TuesdayVibes: post whatever you want and add this hashtag as it's virtually universal!

Notes, Ideas, Metaphors, Story

....
....
....

Related lesson for my audience

....
....
....

Call to action & Hashtags

....
....
....

8th January

#WednesdayWisdom: share a little wisdom or practical advice with your audience using this hashtag

Notes, Ideas, Metaphors, Story

....

....

....

Related lesson for my audience

....

....

....

Call to action & Hashtags

....

....

....

9th January

Post a throwback Thursday

Notes, Ideas, Metaphors, Story

....
....
....

Related lesson for my audience

....
....
....

Call to action & Hashtags

....
....
....

10th January

Post a flashback Friday photo.

....
....
....

Related lesson for my audience

....
....
....

Call to action & Hashtags

....
....
....

11th January

#SaturdayMorning: give your audience a glimpse at how you're spending your Saturday morning.

Notes, Ideas, Metaphors, Story

Related lesson for my audience

Call to action & Hashtags

12th January

#SundayFunday: share how you
are spending your Sunday

Notes, Ideas, Metaphors, Story

....
....
....

Related lesson for my audience

....
....
....

Call to action & Hashtags

....
....
....

13th January

Post some interesting stats or
data about your industry

Notes, Ideas, Metaphors, Story

....
....
....

Related lesson for my audience

....
....
....

Call to action & Hashtags

....
....
....

14th January

Share your favorite resources
[apps, websites, blogs]

Notes, Ideas, Metaphors, Story

....
....
....

Related lesson for my audience

....
....
....

Call to action & Hashtags

....
....
....

15th January

Share a win or success

Notes, Ideas, Metaphors, Story

....
....
....

Related lesson for my audience

....
....
....

Call to action & Hashtags

....
....
....

16th January

Share a loss or a failure

Notes, Ideas, Metaphors, Story

....
....
....

Related lesson for my audience

....
....
....

Call to action & Hashtags

....
....
....

17th January

Post about events you're hosting or going to

Notes, Ideas, Metaphors, Story

....
....
....

Related lesson for my audience

....
....
....

Call to action & Hashtags

....
....
....

18th January

Post where you'll be speaking or where you're making appearances

Notes, Ideas, Metaphors, Story

....
....
....

Related lesson for my audience

....
....
....

Call to action & Hashtags

....
....
....

19th January

Share an unknown feature about
your products or services

Notes, Ideas, Metaphors, Story

....

....

....

Related lesson for my audience

....

....

....

Call to action & Hashtags

....

....

....

20th January

Show someone using your product

Notes, Ideas, Metaphors, Story

....
....
....

Related lesson for my audience

....
....
....

Call to action & Hashtags

....
....
....

21st January

Tell people how you got started or began
learning about your topic in the first place

Notes, Ideas, Metaphors, Story

....
....
....

Related lesson for my audience

....
....
....

Call to action & Hashtags

....
....
....

22nd January

Share what inspired you to create
one of your products or services

Notes, Ideas, Metaphors, Story

....
....
....

Related lesson for my audience

....
....
....

Call to action & Hashtags

....
....
....

23rd January

Shoutout or mention other brands

Notes, Ideas, Metaphors, Story

....
....
....

Related lesson for my audience

....
....
....

Call to action & Hashtags

....
....
....

24th January

Shoutout or mention your clients

Notes, Ideas, Metaphors, Story

....
....
....

Related lesson for my audience

....
....
....

Call to action & Hashtags

....
....
....

25th January

Share a success story - this could be
yours or one of your clients'

Notes, Ideas, Metaphors, Story

....
....
....

Related lesson for my audience

....
....
....

Call to action & Hashtags

....
....
....

26th January

Ask your audience how they found you
or how you met. Better - get them to
share a memory or photo of you!

Notes, Ideas, Metaphors, Story

....
....
....

Related lesson for my audience

....
....
....

Call to action & Hashtags

....
....
....

27th January

Post something seasonal or highlight
an international holiday event

Notes, Ideas, Metaphors, Story

....
....
....

Related lesson for my audience

....
....
....

Call to action & Hashtags

....
....
....

28th January

Host a giveaway, or give something
away for free today

Notes, Ideas, Metaphors, Story

....
....
....

Related lesson for my audience

....
....
....

Call to action & Hashtags

....
....
....

29th January

Ask for book recommendations [or YouTube videos, apps, courses, Music or something else related to your business]

Notes, Ideas, Metaphors, Story

....
....
....

Related lesson for my audience

....
....
....

Call to action & Hashtags

....
....
....

30th January

Share what book you are reading now and
a takeaway that you've got from it so far

Notes, Ideas, Metaphors, Story

....
....
....

Related lesson for my audience

....
....
....

Call to action & Hashtags

....
....
....

31st January

Post about a trip you've taken and something you learned whilst you were there

Notes, Ideas, Metaphors, Story

....
....
....

Related lesson for my audience

....
....
....

Call to action & Hashtags

....
....
....

 **FEBRUARY**

1st February

Talk about mistakes people are
making in your industry

Notes, Ideas, Metaphors, Story

....
....
....

Related lesson for my audience

....
....
....

Call to action & Hashtags

....
....
....

2nd February

Share a story behind your name,
logo, colours or tag line

Notes, Ideas, Metaphors, Story

....
....
....

Related lesson for my audience

....
....
....

Call to action & Hashtags

....
....
....

Share one of your deal breakers in business

Notes, Ideas, Metaphors, Story

....

....

....

Related lesson for my audience

....

....

....

Call to action & Hashtags

....

....

....

4th February

Share your morning routine

Notes, Ideas, Metaphors, Story

....
....
....

Related lesson for my audience

....
....
....

Call to action & Hashtags

....
....
....

5th February

Share your dream vacation destination
and why you want to go there

Notes, Ideas, Metaphors, Story

....
....
....

Related lesson for my audience

....
....
....

Call to action & Hashtags

....
....
....

6th February

Post something you have struggled within your business in the past, or currently

Notes, Ideas, Metaphors, Story

....
....
....

Related lesson for my audience

....
....
....

Call to action & Hashtags

....
....
....

7th February

Do a time-lapse of how you make
a product or deliver a service

Notes, Ideas, Metaphors, Story

....
....
....

Related lesson for my audience

....
....
....

Call to action & Hashtags

....
....
....

8th February

Shoutout to mentor or hero that has encouraged you, inspired you, pushed you or helped you along in your journey (alive or dead).

Notes, Ideas, Metaphors, Story

....
....
....

Related lesson for my audience

....
....
....

Call to action & Hashtags

....
....
....

9th February

Share your favorite self-care tips

Notes, Ideas, Metaphors, Story

....
....
....

Related lesson for my audience

....
....
....

Call to action & Hashtags

....
....
....

10th February

Share what would be in your "Mom/Dad Survival Kit"? If you don't have kids, share what you'd put in your 'Mad Auntie/Uncle Kit' if you were going to watch somebody else's kids

Notes, Ideas, Metaphors, Story

....
....
....

Related lesson for my audience

....
....
....

Call to action & Hashtags

....
....
....

11th February

Announce a new product or service that
you are working on and encourage people
to contribute their thoughts, suggestions
or ideas towards its development

Notes, Ideas, Metaphors, Story

....
....
....

Related lesson for my audience

....
....
....

Call to action & Hashtags

....
....
....

12th February

Share your secret vice or weakness

Notes, Ideas, Metaphors, Story

....
....
....

Related lesson for my audience

....
....
....

Call to action & Hashtags

....
....
....

13th February

Share a discount code

Notes, Ideas, Metaphors, Story

....
....
....

Related lesson for my audience

....
....
....

Call to action & Hashtags

....
....
....

14th February

Share a video or photo of your workspace

Notes, Ideas, Metaphors, Story

....
....
....

Related lesson for my audience

....
....
....

Call to action & Hashtags

....
....
....

15th February

Run a caption contest on a random or funny picture from your camera reel

Notes, Ideas, Metaphors, Story

....
....
....

Related lesson for my audience

....
....
....

Call to action & Hashtags

....
....
....

16th February

Share your business anniversary with
a list of 3 things that you learned in
the past 12 months in business

Notes, Ideas, Metaphors, Story

....

....

....

Related lesson for my audience

....

....

....

Call to action & Hashtags

....

....

....

17th February

Share a personality quiz with the results that you got, and ask your followers to share the results that they got from it too

Notes, Ideas, Metaphors, Story

....
....
....

Related lesson for my audience

....
....
....

Call to action & Hashtags

....
....
....

18th February

Share 3 'get to know me' facts about yourself and ask your followers to share a fact about themselves too

Notes, Ideas, Metaphors, Story

....
....
....

Related lesson for my audience

....
....
....

Call to action & Hashtags

....
....
....

19th February

Post a behind the scenes video of your business

Notes, Ideas, Metaphors, Story

....
....
....

Related lesson for my audience

....
....
....

Call to action & Hashtags

....
....
....

20th February

Post a throwback of you in your business (this could be a photo, video or a written memory)

Notes, Ideas, Metaphors, Story

....

....

....

Related lesson for my audience

....

....

....

Call to action & Hashtags

....

....

....

21st February

Share some valuable information from another influencer and tag them

Notes, Ideas, Metaphors, Story

....

....

....

Related lesson for my audience

....

....

....

Call to action & Hashtags

....

....

....

22nd February

A tip or trick that will solve a simple
challenge your audience might have

Notes, Ideas, Metaphors, Story

....
....
....

Related lesson for my audience

....
....
....

Call to action & Hashtags

....
....
....

23rd February

Post some valuable giveaways (free downloads). These could be your own, or one that you've found from another non-competing business owner.

Notes, Ideas, Metaphors, Story

....
....
....

Related lesson for my audience

....
....
....

Call to action & Hashtags

....
....
....

24th February

Company culture posts (photos, behind the scenes, etc.)

Notes, Ideas, Metaphors, Story

....
....
....

Related lesson for my audience

....
....
....

Call to action & Hashtags

....
....
....

25th February

Post some industry related news with
your opinion or viewpoint on the topic

Notes, Ideas, Metaphors, Story

....

....

....

Related lesson for my audience

....

....

....

Call to action & Hashtags

....

....

....

26th February

Share links to free resources that might
be of interest to your audience

Notes, Ideas, Metaphors, Story

....
....
....

Related lesson for my audience

....
....
....

Call to action & Hashtags

....
....
....

27th February

Share a link to a lead magnet or email
newsletter opt-in that will grow your email list

Notes, Ideas, Metaphors, Story

....
....
....

Related lesson for my audience

....
....
....

Call to action & Hashtags

....
....
....

28th February

Prompt your audience to ask any questions that they have about your topic. I find that asking *'What is your biggest question about [your topic] right now?'* is very effective.

Notes, Ideas, Metaphors, Story

....
....
....

Related lesson for my audience

....
....
....

Call to action & Hashtags

....
....
....

 MARCH

1st March

Share a post about 'what I WISH I knew before I started [your topic]'

Notes, Ideas, Metaphors, Story

....

....

....

Related lesson for my audience

....

....

....

Call to action & Hashtags

....

....

....

Share your views on a mistake that you
are seeing being made in your industry,
and what people should do instead

Notes, Ideas, Metaphors, Story

....

....

....

Related lesson for my audience

....

....

....

Call to action & Hashtags

....

....

....

3rd March

Share a glimpse into your family or home life

....
....
....

Related lesson for my audience

....
....
....

Call to action & Hashtags

....
....
....

4th March

Share something that you have struggled with in your business and how you have (or are) overcoming it

Notes, Ideas, Metaphors, Story

....

....

....

Related lesson for my audience

....

....

....

Call to action & Hashtags

....

....

....

5th March

Share your current business mantra

Notes, Ideas, Metaphors, Story

....
....
....

Related lesson for my audience

....
....
....

Call to action & Hashtags

....
....
....

Share your business accomplishments or milestones from when you started until now. If what you have been through was to become a 'Steps To [Result]' in your industry, what would they be?

Notes, Ideas, Metaphors, Story

....
....
....

Related lesson for my audience

....
....
....

Call to action & Hashtags

....
....
....

7th March

Post a "Fill In The Blank". For example, if you help people lose weight, you might post something like "If I was to be

....
....
....

Related lesson for my audience

....
....
....

Call to action & Hashtags

....
....
....

8th March

International Women's Day –
dedicate this post to women

Notes, Ideas, Metaphors, Story

....

....

....

Related lesson for my audience

....

....

....

Call to action & Hashtags

....

....

....

9th March

Ask your followers how they feel about international women's day, or what they did for international women's day

Notes, Ideas, Metaphors, Story

....
....
....

Related lesson for my audience

....
....
....

Call to action & Hashtags

....
....
....

10th March

Repurpose your old evergreen content. Look back at your old posts and re-publish the ones that had the most amount of engagement.

Notes, Ideas, Metaphors, Story

....

....

....

Related lesson for my audience

....

....

....

Call to action & Hashtags

....

....

....

11th March

Share something you last journalled about.
If you haven't ever journalled, share why

Notes, Ideas, Metaphors, Story

....
....
....

Related lesson for my audience

....
....
....

Call to action & Hashtags

....
....
....

12th March

Share how you manage stress

Notes, Ideas, Metaphors, Story

....
....
....

Related lesson for my audience

....
....
....

Call to action & Hashtags

....
....
....

13th March

Share a meme that makes you laugh

Notes, Ideas, Metaphors, Story

....
....
....

Related lesson for my audience

....
....
....

Call to action & Hashtags

....
....
....

Post a poll on what your next live video should
be about (give them 5 options to choose from)

Notes, Ideas, Metaphors, Story

....

....

....

Related lesson for my audience

....

....

....

Call to action & Hashtags

....

....

....

15th March

Share what your guilty pleasure is

Notes, Ideas, Metaphors, Story

....

....

....

Related lesson for my audience

....

....

....

Call to action & Hashtags

....

....

....

16th March

Share your favourite podcast at the
moment and why you like it

Notes, Ideas, Metaphors, Story

....
....
....

Related lesson for my audience

....
....
....

Call to action & Hashtags

....
....
....

17th March

Share your favorite YouTube channel
at the moment and why you like it

Notes, Ideas, Metaphors, Story

....

....

....

Related lesson for my audience

....

....

....

Call to action & Hashtags

....

....

....

18th March

Recommend the most helpful online courses
that you've taken in the past 12 months

Notes, Ideas, Metaphors, Story

....
....
....

Related lesson for my audience

....
....
....

Call to action & Hashtags

....
....
....

19th March

Link to a tool/resource you can't live without
to do your job or run your business

Notes, Ideas, Metaphors, Story

....

....

....

Related lesson for my audience

....

....

....

Call to action & Hashtags

....

....

....

20th March

Share a product or service you love and
your audience will benefit from

Notes, Ideas, Metaphors, Story

....
....
....

Related lesson for my audience

....
....
....

Call to action & Hashtags

....
....
....

21st March

Share what you do to motivate yourself
when you've lost your mojo

Notes, Ideas, Metaphors, Story

....
....
....

Related lesson for my audience

....
....
....

Call to action & Hashtags

....
....
....

22nd March

Share your time saving tips or
a life-hack that you use

Notes, Ideas, Metaphors, Story

....
....
....

Related lesson for my audience

....
....
....

Call to action & Hashtags

....
....
....

23rd March

Share a tip you have about
money saving or earning

Notes, Ideas, Metaphors, Story

....

....

....

Related lesson for my audience

....

....

....

Call to action & Hashtags

....

....

....

24th March

Share an interesting statistic in your industry

Notes, Ideas, Metaphors, Story

....
....
....

Related lesson for my audience

....
....
....

Call to action & Hashtags

....
....
....

25th March

Share a post celebrating the number of followers that you currently have and thanking everyone

Notes, Ideas, Metaphors, Story

....
....
....

Related lesson for my audience

....
....
....

Call to action & Hashtags

....
....
....

26th March

Talk about your big 'why'. Why you do what you do, why you started your business, why you get up every morning.

Notes, Ideas, Metaphors, Story

....

....

....

Related lesson for my audience

....

....

....

Call to action & Hashtags

....

....

....

27th March

Recommend someone else they should follow

Notes, Ideas, Metaphors, Story

....
....
....

Related lesson for my audience

....
....
....

Call to action & Hashtags

....
....
....

28th March

Share an ICYMI (in case you missed it) post
to an old blog post, YouTube video or
livestream that you previously posted

Notes, Ideas, Metaphors, Story

....

....

....

Related lesson for my audience

....

....

....

Call to action & Hashtags

....

....

....

29th March

Share a theory, philosophy or psychological concept around your topic

Notes, Ideas, Metaphors, Story

....
....
....

Related lesson for my audience

....
....
....

Call to action & Hashtags

....
....
....

Make a friendly selfie to let your followers
know the person behind the brand

Notes, Ideas, Metaphors, Story

....
....
....

Related lesson for my audience

....
....
....

Call to action & Hashtags

....
....
....

31st March

Go behind the scenes and share what happens on the unseen side of your business

Notes, Ideas, Metaphors, Story

....

....

....

Related lesson for my audience

....

....

....

Call to action & Hashtags

....

....

....

 **APRIL**

1st April

April Fool's Day – create a funny
and hilarious post for this day

Notes, Ideas, Metaphors, Story

....
....
....

Related lesson for my audience

....
....
....

Call to action & Hashtags

....
....
....

2nd April

Ask your followers what makes them laugh, or what the funniest thing they witnessed on April Fool's day was

Notes, Ideas, Metaphors, Story

....
....
....

Related lesson for my audience

....
....
....

Call to action & Hashtags

....
....
....

3rd April

Share an educational or informative article
related to your niche topic or industry

Notes, Ideas, Metaphors, Story

....
....
....

Related lesson for my audience

....
....
....

Call to action & Hashtags

....
....
....

Answer a question that you get asked a lot

Notes, Ideas, Metaphors, Story

....
....
....

Related lesson for my audience

....
....
....

Call to action & Hashtags

....
....
....

5th April

Reveal what's currently working well for
your customers or your business

Notes, Ideas, Metaphors, Story

....
....
....

Related lesson for my audience

....
....
....

Call to action & Hashtags

....
....
....

6th April

Show an award or accolade you or your business has received. If you haven't won an award, ask your audience what they think you'd win an award for if you were to get one

Notes, Ideas, Metaphors, Story

....
....
....

Related lesson for my audience

....
....
....

Call to action & Hashtags

....
....
....

7th April

Make or share a how-to video detailing the steps on how to do something very specific that appeals to your ideal customer

Notes, Ideas, Metaphors, Story

....
....
....

Related lesson for my audience

....
....
....

Call to action & Hashtags

....
....
....

8th April

Announce a live one-on-one coaching session you'll give or discount to one person who comments on this post

Notes, Ideas, Metaphors, Story

....

....

....

Related lesson for my audience

....

....

....

Call to action & Hashtags

....

....

....

9th April

Select one person from the comments
to your previous post and coach them -
announcing who won to everyone else

Notes, Ideas, Metaphors, Story

....
....
....

Related lesson for my audience

....
....
....

Call to action & Hashtags

....
....
....

10th April

Share a mistake you typically see your customers or competitors make - and what they should be doing instead

Notes, Ideas, Metaphors, Story

....

....

....

Related lesson for my audience

....

....

....

Call to action & Hashtags

....

....

....

11th April

Share a software, digital tool or app
that you have used a lot lately

Notes, Ideas, Metaphors, Story

....
....
....

Related lesson for my audience

....
....
....

Call to action & Hashtags

....
....
....

12th April

Share a fun fact about your industry or niche

Notes, Ideas, Metaphors, Story

....
....
....

Related lesson for my audience

....
....
....

Call to action & Hashtags

....
....
....

13th April

Post an infographic with helpful tips
or information for your audience. You
can design your own using Canva, get a
graphic designer on Fiverr to make one
for you, or share somebody else's

Notes, Ideas, Metaphors, Story

....
....
....

Related lesson for my audience

....
....
....

Call to action & Hashtags

....
....
....

14th April

Share a tip that will help your audience be
more efficient and save time in your field

Notes, Ideas, Metaphors, Story

....

....

....

Related lesson for my audience

....

....

....

Call to action & Hashtags

....

....

....

15th April

Reveal a tip that will help your
audience save money

Notes, Ideas, Metaphors, Story

....

....

....

Related lesson for my audience

....

....

....

Call to action & Hashtags

....

....

....

16th April

Share a super simple hack to a common problem your customer faces

Notes, Ideas, Metaphors, Story

....
....
....

Related lesson for my audience

....
....
....

Call to action & Hashtags

....
....
....

17th April

Open a page from a book near you and share
a tip from it; then relate that tip to your topic

Notes, Ideas, Metaphors, Story

....

....

....

Related lesson for my audience

....

....

....

Call to action & Hashtags

....

....

....

18th April

Make a poll to test new ideas with your audience

Notes, Ideas, Metaphors, Story

....
....
....

Related lesson for my audience

....
....
....

Call to action & Hashtags

....
....
....

Pick up the object closest to your left
hand and share how it is metaphorically
similar to your audience, your topic or
a problem your audience faces

Notes, Ideas, Metaphors, Story

....

....

....

Related lesson for my audience

....

....

....

Call to action & Hashtags

....

....

....

20th April

Encourage your followers to share
their predictions about a trend within
your industry or a current event

Notes, Ideas, Metaphors, Story

....
....
....

Related lesson for my audience

....
....
....

Call to action & Hashtags

....
....
....

21st April

Tell about an influencer who
inspires and motivates you

Notes, Ideas, Metaphors, Story

....
....
....

Related lesson for my audience

....
....
....

Call to action & Hashtags

....
....
....

22nd April

Share something about how it feels
to be a man/woman/non-binary
business owner in your industry

Notes, Ideas, Metaphors, Story

....
....
....

Related lesson for my audience

....
....
....

Call to action & Hashtags

....
....
....

23rd April

Share a current industry trend in
your field, or something that is 'viral'
related to your business topic

Notes, Ideas, Metaphors, Story

....

....

....

Related lesson for my audience

....

....

....

Call to action & Hashtags

....

....

....

Share a prediction post about your industry.
What do you think might happen in your field
in the short term and long term future? Or, do
you think it will always be the same? Why?

Notes, Ideas, Metaphors, Story

....

....

....

Related lesson for my audience

....

....

....

Call to action & Hashtags

....

....

....

25th April

Post a photo from some of your fan's profiles and share how you are proud of them or inspired by them. They will be amazed!

Notes, Ideas, Metaphors, Story

....

....

....

Related lesson for my audience

....

....

....

Call to action & Hashtags

....

....

....

26th April

If you have a favorite charity or cause you support, share it with your audience and tell a story about why this initiative is important to you

Notes, Ideas, Metaphors, Story

....

....

....

Related lesson for my audience

....

....

....

Call to action & Hashtags

....

....

....

27th April

Feature a customer by sharing a video interview
of how and why they became your client

Notes, Ideas, Metaphors, Story

....
....
....

Related lesson for my audience

....
....
....

Call to action & Hashtags

....
....
....

28th April

Interview an expert or influencer in your niche and share the video as a post

....
....
....

Related lesson for my audience

....
....
....

Call to action & Hashtags

....
....
....

29th April

#TBT (Throwback Thursday): use this hashtag (one of the oldest and most widely used daily ones!) to post an old photo (the older the better) and tell about that time in your life

Notes, Ideas, Metaphors, Story

....

....

....

Related lesson for my audience

....

....

....

Call to action & Hashtags

....

....

....

30th April

#FridayNight: show why your
Friday night is so fun!

Notes, Ideas, Metaphors, Story

....

....

....

Related lesson for my audience

....

....

....

Call to action & Hashtags

....

....

....

MAY

1st May

International Day of Happiness – tell your audience why you're happy/what makes you happy, and ask about what makes them happy

Notes, Ideas, Metaphors, Story

....

....

....

Related lesson for my audience

....

....

....

Call to action & Hashtags

....

....

....

2nd May

World's Poetry Day – tell your audience
how you feel about poetry, and ask for their
opinion. Better yet, create a nice, funny
or deep poem about your industry

Notes, Ideas, Metaphors, Story

....
....
....

Related lesson for my audience

....
....
....

Call to action & Hashtags

....
....
....

@Mention a Follower: if you have a
follower who engages regularly with your
content, give them a shout out using the
@mention feature and thank them

Notes, Ideas, Metaphors, Story

....
....
....

Related lesson for my audience

....
....
....

Call to action & Hashtags

....
....
....

@Mention an Influencer: if there's an influencer in your niche who you'd like to develop a relationship with, @mention them in a post and share something you've learned from them

Notes, Ideas, Metaphors, Story

....

....

....

Related lesson for my audience

....

....

....

Call to action & Hashtags

....

....

....

5th May

Thank your followers for staying with you!

Notes, Ideas, Metaphors, Story

....
....
....

Related lesson for my audience

....
....
....

Call to action & Hashtags

....
....
....

6th May

Share your newest content: the latest blog post, podcast, or video

Notes, Ideas, Metaphors, Story

....
....
....

Related lesson for my audience

....
....
....

Call to action & Hashtags

....
....
....

7th May

Repurpose old content and dust off some old blog post (don't forget to update the images and headline!)

Notes, Ideas, Metaphors, Story

....
....
....

Related lesson for my audience

....
....
....

Call to action & Hashtags

....
....
....

8th May

Share your most popular piece of content

Notes, Ideas, Metaphors, Story

....

....

....

Related lesson for my audience

....

....

....

Call to action & Hashtags

....

....

....

9th May

Deliver a post or video with the title
'This could change your life'

Notes, Ideas, Metaphors, Story

....

....

....

Related lesson for my audience

....

....

....

Call to action & Hashtags

....

....

....

10th May

Use a changeable letter sign, white board or piece of paper to make a photo of fun/creative/inspirational note that you can photograph and share

Notes, Ideas, Metaphors, Story

....
....
....

Related lesson for my audience

....
....
....

Call to action & Hashtags

....
....
....

Make a statement: take a photo of a t-shirt, coffee mug, or another item with a fun quote or saying on it

Notes, Ideas, Metaphors, Story

....
....
....

Related lesson for my audience

....
....
....

Call to action & Hashtags

....
....
....

Promote your newsletter by letting your audience know what's so special about it and encourage your audience to subscribe

Notes, Ideas, Metaphors, Story

....

....

....

Related lesson for my audience

....

....

....

Call to action & Hashtags

....

....

....

13th May

Deliver a post titled 'I wish I
knew this when I started'

Notes, Ideas, Metaphors, Story

....

....

....

Related lesson for my audience

....

....

....

Call to action & Hashtags

....

....

....

14th May

Easter – Create a post about this holiday and any tips that relate your topic to Easter

Notes, Ideas, Metaphors, Story

....

....

....

Related lesson for my audience

....

....

....

Call to action & Hashtags

....

....

....

15th May

Run a contest and encourage your audience
to share your content with others or
create a specific post on social media

Notes, Ideas, Metaphors, Story

....
....
....

Related lesson for my audience

....
....
....

Call to action & Hashtags

....
....
....

16th May

World's health day – make a post
about health or a healthy lifestyle

Notes, Ideas, Metaphors, Story

....
....
....

Related lesson for my audience

....
....
....

Call to action & Hashtags

....
....
....

17th May

Ask your followers whether they
follow a healthy lifestyle or not

Notes, Ideas, Metaphors, Story

....
....
....

Related lesson for my audience

....
....
....

Call to action & Hashtags

....
....
....

Announce your tomorrow's
Follower-Only Flash Sale

Notes, Ideas, Metaphors, Story

....

....

....

Related lesson for my audience

....

....

....

Call to action & Hashtags

....

....

....

19th May

Run a 1-day flash sale ONLY for
your social media followers

Notes, Ideas, Metaphors, Story

....
....
....

Related lesson for my audience

....
....
....

Call to action & Hashtags

....
....
....

Promote the launch of your
new product or service

Notes, Ideas, Metaphors, Story

....
....
....

Related lesson for my audience

....
....
....

Call to action & Hashtags

....
....
....

21st May

Whatever milestone you've hit, celebrate it on social media and share it with your audience

Notes, Ideas, Metaphors, Story

....

....

....

Related lesson for my audience

....

....

....

Call to action & Hashtags

....

....

....

22nd May

Share a tweet you like

Notes, Ideas, Metaphors, Story

....
....
....

Related lesson for my audience

....
....
....

Call to action & Hashtags

....
....
....

22nd May

Talk about your bucket list

Notes, Ideas, Metaphors, Story

....
....
....

Related lesson for my audience

....
....
....

Call to action & Hashtags

....
....
....

23rd May

If you have employees who help make your business great, tell the world about them!

Notes, Ideas, Metaphors, Story

....
....
....

Related lesson for my audience

....
....
....

Call to action & Hashtags

....
....
....

24th May

As your audience grows on social media,
reintroduce yourself and your business

Notes, Ideas, Metaphors, Story

....
....
....

Related lesson for my audience

....
....
....

Call to action & Hashtags

....
....
....

25th May

Post something seasonal

Related lesson for my audience

Call to action & Hashtags

Share an attention-grabbing statistic

Notes, Ideas, Metaphors, Story

....
....
....

Related lesson for my audience

....
....
....

Call to action & Hashtags

....
....
....

Correct a common misconception
that's related to your industry

Notes, Ideas, Metaphors, Story

....
....
....

Related lesson for my audience

....
....
....

Call to action & Hashtags

....
....
....

28th May

International Mother Earth Day – share
your love to Earth with your subscribers

Notes, Ideas, Metaphors, Story

....

....

....

Related lesson for my audience

....

....

....

Call to action & Hashtags

....

....

....

29th May

Give a shout out to another local business or organization

Notes, Ideas, Metaphors, Story

....

....

....

Related lesson for my audience

....

....

....

Call to action & Hashtags

....

....

....

Invite people to join your mailing list

Notes, Ideas, Metaphors, Story

....
....
....

Related lesson for my audience

....
....
....

Call to action & Hashtags

....
....
....

 JUNE

1st June

Ask your audience what their
biggest struggle in business is

Notes, Ideas, Metaphors, Story

....
....
....

Related lesson for my audience

....
....
....

Call to action & Hashtags

....
....
....

2nd June

Share how to create & write down your goals

Notes, Ideas, Metaphors, Story

....
....
....

Related lesson for my audience

....
....
....

Call to action & Hashtags

....
....
....

3rd June

Challenge your audience to post every day for 30 days and give them a free Social Media calendar

Notes, Ideas, Metaphors, Story

....

....

....

Related lesson for my audience

....

....

....

Call to action & Hashtags

....

....

....

4th June

Talk about your products and
how they help people

Notes, Ideas, Metaphors, Story

....
....
....

Related lesson for my audience

....
....
....

Call to action & Hashtags

....
....
....

5th June

Share someone else's inspiring story

Notes, Ideas, Metaphors, Story

....
....
....

Related lesson for my audience

....
....
....

Call to action & Hashtags

....
....
....

Give away coupon codes

Notes, Ideas, Metaphors, Story

....
....
....

Related lesson for my audience

....
....
....

Call to action & Hashtags

....
....
....

Create fill in the blank posts

Notes, Ideas, Metaphors, Story

....
....
....

Related lesson for my audience

....
....
....

Call to action & Hashtags

....
....
....
....

8th June

Create a challenge related to your niche

Notes, Ideas, Metaphors, Story

....
....
....

Related lesson for my audience

....
....
....

Call to action & Hashtags

....
....
....

9th June

Share a quote (graphics) and ask your
audience what they think about it

Notes, Ideas, Metaphors, Story

....
....
....

Related lesson for my audience

....
....
....

Call to action & Hashtags

....
....
....

Ask followers what you should post next

Notes, Ideas, Metaphors, Story

....
....
....

Related lesson for my audience

....
....
....

Call to action & Hashtags

....
....
....

11th June

Challenge your audience to share their 3 goals
and achieve at least one of them in a week

Notes, Ideas, Metaphors, Story

....

....

....

Related lesson for my audience

....

....

....

Call to action & Hashtags

....

....

....

Ask your audience to share their favorite quote

Notes, Ideas, Metaphors, Story

....
....
....

Related lesson for my audience

....
....
....

Call to action & Hashtags

....
....
....

Create a 5-day mini-course about
a specific topic in your niche

Notes, Ideas, Metaphors, Story

....

....

....

Related lesson for my audience

....

....

....

Call to action & Hashtags

....

....

....

14th June

Fill in the blank: My favorite blog
is_____. Because….

Notes, Ideas, Metaphors, Story

....
....
....

Related lesson for my audience

....
....
....

Call to action & Hashtags

....
....
....

15th June

Fill in the blank: I'm inspired by_____. Because…..

Notes, Ideas, Metaphors, Story

....
....
....

Related lesson for my audience

....
....
....

Call to action & Hashtags

....
....
....

16th June

Fill in the blank: One of my all-time favorite books is _____. Because….

Notes, Ideas, Metaphors, Story

....
....
....

Related lesson for my audience

....
....
....

Call to action & Hashtags

....
....
....

Fill in the blank: If I could be anywhere right now, it would be_____. Because…

Notes, Ideas, Metaphors, Story

....
....
....

Related lesson for my audience

....
....
....

Call to action & Hashtags

....
....
....

18th June

Ask your followers: Would you rather have 5 close friends or 10,000 Facebook friends, and why?

Notes, Ideas, Metaphors, Story

....
....
....

Related lesson for my audience

....
....
....

Call to action & Hashtags

....
....
....

Ask your followers: Would you rather have
$100,000 in real money or $1,000,000
in Amazon gift cards, and why?

Notes, Ideas, Metaphors, Story

....

....

....

Related lesson for my audience

....

....

....

Call to action & Hashtags

....

....

....

Ask your followers: Would you rather be famous or the best friend of someone famous, and why?

Notes, Ideas, Metaphors, Story

....
....
....

Related lesson for my audience

....
....
....

Call to action & Hashtags

....
....
....

21st June

Ask your followers: What is your favorite time of the year, and why? Make sure you share yours!

Notes, Ideas, Metaphors, Story

....
....
....

Related lesson for my audience

....
....
....

Call to action & Hashtags

....
....
....

Ask your followers: What is your biggest fear?

Notes, Ideas, Metaphors, Story

....
....
....

Related lesson for my audience

....
....
....

Call to action & Hashtags

....
....
....

23rd June

Ask your followers: What was the last thing you got really excited about? Make sure you share yours!

Notes, Ideas, Metaphors, Story

....
....
....

Related lesson for my audience

....
....
....

Call to action & Hashtags

....
....
....

24th June

Ask your followers: What is your superpower?

Notes, Ideas, Metaphors, Story

....
....
....

Related lesson for my audience

....
....
....

Call to action & Hashtags

....
....
....

25th June

Ask your followers: What is the best
compliment you have ever received?
Make sure you share yours

Notes, Ideas, Metaphors, Story

....
....
....

Related lesson for my audience

....
....
....

Call to action & Hashtags

....
....
....

26th June

Ask your followers: If you could only have
one app on your phone, what would
it be? Make sure you share yours

Notes, Ideas, Metaphors, Story

....

....

....

Related lesson for my audience

....

....

....

Call to action & Hashtags

....

....

....

27th June

Ask your followers: What one thing do
you hope to accomplish this week?
Make sure you share yours

Notes, Ideas, Metaphors, Story

....

....

....

Related lesson for my audience

....

....

....

Call to action & Hashtags

....

....

....

Ask your followers: If you were a superhero, who would you be, and why?

Notes, Ideas, Metaphors, Story

....

....

....

Related lesson for my audience

....

....

....

Call to action & Hashtags

....

....

....

Ask your followers: What are you
most thankful for today?

Notes, Ideas, Metaphors, Story

....
....
....

Related lesson for my audience

....
....
....

Call to action & Hashtags

....
....
....

30th June

Ask your followers: What's the one movie you could watch over and over again? Make sure you share yours!

Notes, Ideas, Metaphors, Story

....
....
....

Related lesson for my audience

....
....
....

Call to action & Hashtags

....
....
....

JULY

1st July

Welcome new followers and thank them
for joining your group or page

Notes, Ideas, Metaphors, Story

....
....
....

Related lesson for my audience

....
....
....

Call to action & Hashtags

....
....
....

2nd July

Share a post on how long it takes to [something your audience want to know about your topic]

Notes, Ideas, Metaphors, Story

....
....
....

Related lesson for my audience

....
....
....

Call to action & Hashtags

....
....
....

3rd July

Deliver a post titled 'X things that life has taught me so far this year'

Notes, Ideas, Metaphors, Story

....
....
....

Related lesson for my audience

....
....
....

Call to action & Hashtags

....
....
....

4th July

Explain how you prepare for
the day or week ahead

Notes, Ideas, Metaphors, Story

....
....
....

Related lesson for my audience

....
....
....

Call to action & Hashtags

....
....
....

5th July

Share all the things you do daily,
or a list of your good habits

Notes, Ideas, Metaphors, Story

....
....
....

Related lesson for my audience

....
....
....

Call to action & Hashtags

....
....
....

6th July

Share your top favourite tools and apps
that help you get or stay organised

Notes, Ideas, Metaphors, Story

....
....
....

Related lesson for my audience

....
....
....

Call to action & Hashtags

....
....
....

7th July

Deliver a post titled 'The best
investment I ever made'

Notes, Ideas, Metaphors, Story

....
....
....

Related lesson for my audience

....
....
....

Call to action & Hashtags

....
....
....

8th July

Share your vision board or
explain your dream life

Notes, Ideas, Metaphors, Story

....

....

....

Related lesson for my audience

....

....

....

Call to action & Hashtags

....

....

....

9th July

Answer a frequently asked question in your topic

Notes, Ideas, Metaphors, Story

....
....
....

Related lesson for my audience

....
....
....

Call to action & Hashtags

....
....
....

10th July

Talk about what you stand for, your morals,
your values, what you think is important
in a [target audiences'] morals

Notes, Ideas, Metaphors, Story

....
....
....

Related lesson for my audience

....
....
....

Call to action & Hashtags

....
....
....

11th July

Share a trip, journey or other
destination you are going to next

Notes, Ideas, Metaphors, Story

....
....
....

Related lesson for my audience

....
....
....

Call to action & Hashtags

....
....
....

12th July

Go live interviewing another expert in a topic that would interest your audience

Notes, Ideas, Metaphors, Story

....

....

....

Related lesson for my audience

....

....

....

Call to action & Hashtags

....

....

....

Pick up an item to your right. Share a post about how the item is metaphorically similar to your target audience, or a problem they have.

Notes, Ideas, Metaphors, Story

....

....

....

Related lesson for my audience

....

....

....

Call to action & Hashtags

....

....

....

14th July

Create a "Letter to my younger self"

Notes, Ideas, Metaphors, Story

....

....

....

Related lesson for my audience

....

....

....

Call to action & Hashtags

....

....

....

15th July

Share a post about your pets. If you don't have pets, share a post about a pet you'd love to have an why

Notes, Ideas, Metaphors, Story

....
....
....

Related lesson for my audience

....
....
....

Call to action & Hashtags

....
....
....

Talk about your favorite things
to do in your spare time

Notes, Ideas, Metaphors, Story

....
....
....

Related lesson for my audience

....
....
....

Call to action & Hashtags

....
....
....

What are your top tips for productivity?

Notes, Ideas, Metaphors, Story

....
....
....

Related lesson for my audience

....
....
....

Call to action & Hashtags

....
....
....

Talk about a weekend, holiday or event that went really badly - and what you learned from it

Notes, Ideas, Metaphors, Story

....
....
....

Related lesson for my audience

....
....
....

Call to action & Hashtags

....
....
....

19th July

Ask followers how they spend their time off

Notes, Ideas, Metaphors, Story

....
....
....

Related lesson for my audience

....
....
....

Call to action & Hashtags

....
....
....

20th July

Ask your followers about the country they are from

Notes, Ideas, Metaphors, Story

....
....
....

Related lesson for my audience

....
....
....

Call to action & Hashtags

....
....
....

21st July

Celebrate your blogging anniversary. How many weeks, months or years have you been blogging today? Do you wish you'd done more? How has it impacted your business? Are you planning to start if you haven't yet?

Notes, Ideas, Metaphors, Story

....

....

....

Related lesson for my audience

....

....

....

Call to action & Hashtags

....

....

....

22nd July

Announce a win, success or something you checked off of your to-do list this past week. Ask your audience what theirs is too.

Notes, Ideas, Metaphors, Story

....

....

....

Related lesson for my audience

....

....

....

Call to action & Hashtags

....

....

....

23rd July

Share what you're currently listening
to on podcasts or Audible. Ask your
audience to share theirs too

Notes, Ideas, Metaphors, Story

....
....
....

Related lesson for my audience

....
....
....

Call to action & Hashtags

....
....
....

24th July

Take a screenshot of your Kindle app and share it. Ask your audience what they are reading right now too.

Notes, Ideas, Metaphors, Story

....

....

....

Related lesson for my audience

....

....

....

Call to action & Hashtags

....

....

....

25th July

Share a screenshot of your home screen
on your phone and how you've organised
your apps. Yes, even if it is a hilarious mess.
Ask your audience to share theirs too.

Notes, Ideas, Metaphors, Story

....
....
....

Related lesson for my audience

....
....
....

Call to action & Hashtags

....
....
....

26th July

Share your goals for the upcoming month
and ask your audience to share their too

Notes, Ideas, Metaphors, Story

....
....
....

Related lesson for my audience

....
....
....

Call to action & Hashtags

....
....
....

27th July

Create a checklist or cheat sheet that your followers can download. Make sure that you get their email address in exchange

Notes, Ideas, Metaphors, Story

....
....
....

Related lesson for my audience

....
....
....

Call to action & Hashtags

....
....
....

28th July

Take a popular topic in your industry
and write a long detailed post on it

Notes, Ideas, Metaphors, Story

....

....

....

Related lesson for my audience

....

....

....

Call to action & Hashtags

....

....

....

29th July

Share your viewpoints on a current affair in your industry (nothing too controversial)

Notes, Ideas, Metaphors, Story

....
....
....

Related lesson for my audience

....
....
....

Call to action & Hashtags

....
....
....

Deliver a post titled 'Why i nearly quit/gave up on X, and why I am so glad that I didn't'

Notes, Ideas, Metaphors, Story

....

....

....

Related lesson for my audience

....

....

....

Call to action & Hashtags

....

....

....

31st July

Show your favorite hacks and tools now. You may want to refer to the last time you posted about this and let people know that you have some new finds!

Notes, Ideas, Metaphors, Story

....

....

....

Related lesson for my audience

....

....

....

Call to action & Hashtags

....

....

....

 AUGUST

1st August

Encourage your audience to opt-in to an email course or challenge to help build your list

Notes, Ideas, Metaphors, Story

....
....
....

Related lesson for my audience

....
....
....

Call to action & Hashtags

....
....
....

2nd August

Give positive words of encouragement
and motivation in your topic

....
....
....

Related lesson for my audience

....
....
....

Call to action & Hashtags

....
....
....

3rd August

Share a funny joke (be careful about anything that might be offensive)

Notes, Ideas, Metaphors, Story

....

....

....

Related lesson for my audience

....

....

....

Call to action & Hashtags

....

....

....

4th August

Ask your followers to set larger goals for the year

....
....
....

Related lesson for my audience

....
....
....

Call to action & Hashtags

....
....
....

5th August

Ask your audience what they want
to see more of from you

Notes, Ideas, Metaphors, Story

....
....
....

Related lesson for my audience

....
....
....

Call to action & Hashtags

....
....
....

6th August

'Before and After': Compare something in your life before and after, then and now and relate it back to growth in your topic

Notes, Ideas, Metaphors, Story

....

....

....

Related lesson for my audience

....

....

....

Call to action & Hashtags

....

....

....

7th August

Share a mantra or affirmations you say to keep
yourself motivated to accomplish your own goals

Notes, Ideas, Metaphors, Story

....
....
....

Related lesson for my audience

....
....
....

Call to action & Hashtags

....
....
....

8th August

Show your morning ritual or helpful nightly routine to help you stay energized, focused, healthy, or positive

Notes, Ideas, Metaphors, Story

....
....
....

Related lesson for my audience

....
....
....

Call to action & Hashtags

....
....
....

9th August

Express your gratitude to anyone (customer, mentor, employee, parther, friend).

Notes, Ideas, Metaphors, Story

....
....
....

Related lesson for my audience

....
....
....

Call to action & Hashtags

....
....
....

10th August

Share a testimonial, quote, case study
or video from a satisfied customer

Notes, Ideas, Metaphors, Story

....

....

....

Related lesson for my audience

....

....

....

Call to action & Hashtags

....

....

....

11th August

Talk about something that made
you laugh this week

Notes, Ideas, Metaphors, Story

....
....
....

Related lesson for my audience

....
....
....

Call to action & Hashtags

....
....
....

12th August

Share a memory from your childhood -
added points for a pic of you as a kid!

Notes, Ideas, Metaphors, Story

....
....
....

Related lesson for my audience

....
....
....

Call to action & Hashtags

....
....
....

13th August

Talk about a defining moment in your life

Notes, Ideas, Metaphors, Story

....
....
....

Related lesson for my audience

....
....
....

Call to action & Hashtags

....
....
....

14th August

Post a photo with your significant
other or a close friend

Notes, Ideas, Metaphors, Story

....
....
....

Related lesson for my audience

....
....
....

Call to action & Hashtags

....
....
....

15th August

Post a photo of your bookshelf or book pile
and encourage your audience to do the same

Notes, Ideas, Metaphors, Story

....
....
....

Related lesson for my audience

....
....
....

Call to action & Hashtags

....
....
....

16th August

Ask your audience about their friends

Notes, Ideas, Metaphors, Story

....
....
....

Related lesson for my audience

....
....
....

Call to action & Hashtags

....
....
....

17th August

Share a photo of an item that you cherish, and talk about why it means so much to you

Notes, Ideas, Metaphors, Story

'23 - Did 'Meet the Owners" Post - GOOD REACTION!!

Related lesson for my audience

Call to action & Hashtags

18th August

Share a photo of a project you're
currently working on

Notes, Ideas, Metaphors, Story

....

....

....

Related lesson for my audience

....

....

....

Call to action & Hashtags

....

....

....

19th August

Host an "Ask Me Anything" live video

Notes, Ideas, Metaphors, Story

....
....
....

Related lesson for my audience

....
....
....

Call to action & Hashtags

....
....
....

20th August

Talk about something that didn't go
perfectly to plan for you this week,
and what you learned from it

Notes, Ideas, Metaphors, Story

....
....
....

Related lesson for my audience

....
....
....

Call to action & Hashtags

....
....
....

21st August

Pick up and book near you, turn
to the 59th page and share a tip or
message from it to your audience

Notes, Ideas, Metaphors, Story

....
....
....

Related lesson for my audience

....
....
....

Call to action & Hashtags

....
....
....

22nd August

Share your morning workout

Notes, Ideas, Metaphors, Story

....
....
....

Related lesson for my audience

....
....
....

Call to action & Hashtags

....
....
....

23rd August

Share your relaxation spot

Notes, Ideas, Metaphors, Story

....
....
....

Related lesson for my audience

....
....
....

Call to action & Hashtags

....
....
....

24th August

Share a personality trait or characteristic that you find inspiring or attractive in people

Notes, Ideas, Metaphors, Story

....
....
....

Related lesson for my audience

....
....
....

Call to action & Hashtags

....
....
....

25th August

Talk about the last thing that you purchased, why you bought it and whether it was a good purchase or not

Notes, Ideas, Metaphors, Story

....

....

....

Related lesson for my audience

....

....

....

Call to action & Hashtags

....

....

....

26th August

Create a VIP list and each week choose
1 winner (send them a special gift)

Notes, Ideas, Metaphors, Story

....
....
....

Related lesson for my audience

....
....
....

Call to action & Hashtags

....
....
....

27th August

Challenge your audience to post for 30 days about something that they love (why not become an affiliate of mine and get them to join my #30Days30Tips challenge?!)

Notes, Ideas, Metaphors, Story

....

....

....

Related lesson for my audience

....

....

....

Call to action & Hashtags

....

....

....

28th August

Challenge your audience to write and share 3 of their own goals with their own audience

Notes, Ideas, Metaphors, Story

....
....
....

Related lesson for my audience

....
....
....

Call to action & Hashtags

....
....
....

29th August

Make a 5 day mini-challenge in your topic. You can get a FREE Course Creation Starter Kit from me here: www.sarahcordiner.com/starterkit

Notes, Ideas, Metaphors, Story

....
....
....

Related lesson for my audience

....
....
....

Call to action & Hashtags

....
....
....

30th August

Visit a garden or go out in nature and
show people around via livestream

Notes, Ideas, Metaphors, Story

....

....

....

Related lesson for my audience

....

....

....

Call to action & Hashtags

....

....

....

31st August

Talk about the last time you did something new, or experienced something for the very first time

Notes, Ideas, Metaphors, Story

....

....

....

Related lesson for my audience

....

....

....

Call to action & Hashtags

....

....

....

 **SEPTEMBER**

Deliver a post titled 'a big myth about [your topic]

Notes, Ideas, Metaphors, Story

....
....
....

Related lesson for my audience

....
....
....

Call to action & Hashtags

....
....
....

2nd September

Answer another common question
that you get in your line of work

Notes, Ideas, Metaphors, Story

....
....
....

Related lesson for my audience

....
....
....

Call to action & Hashtags

....
....
....

3rd September

Share a post about how you feel when you get lost, and offer a tip of advice to your audience for when they are feeling lost

Notes, Ideas, Metaphors, Story

....

....

....

Related lesson for my audience

....

....

....

Call to action & Hashtags

....

....

....

4th September

Share a post about leadership in your industry

Notes, Ideas, Metaphors, Story

....
....
....

Related lesson for my audience

....
....
....

Call to action & Hashtags

....
....
....

5th September

Be open about some bad habits you've broken

Notes, Ideas, Metaphors, Story

....

....

....

Related lesson for my audience

....

....

....

Call to action & Hashtags

....

....

....

6th September

Share changes you've made in your
business recently - or plan to make soon

Notes, Ideas, Metaphors, Story

....
....
....

Related lesson for my audience

....
....
....

Call to action & Hashtags

....
....
....

7th September

Talk about a current event

Notes, Ideas, Metaphors, Story

....
....
....

Related lesson for my audience

....
....
....

Call to action & Hashtags

....
....
....

8th September

Pick up another book, turn to page 114 and share a thought, post, tip or reflection on what you find

Notes, Ideas, Metaphors, Story

....
....
....

Related lesson for my audience

....
....
....

Call to action & Hashtags

....
....
....

9th September

Scroll through your camera roll to the
17th photo and share what it is about

Notes, Ideas, Metaphors, Story

....

....

....

Related lesson for my audience

....

....

....

Call to action & Hashtags

....

....

....

10th September

Create a grid layout of photos related
to your topic, products or services

....
....
....

Related lesson for my audience

....
....
....

Call to action & Hashtags

....
....
....

11th September

Share something you recently indulged
in - and how it in some way relates (directly
or metaphorically) to your topic

Notes, Ideas, Metaphors, Story

....
....
....

Related lesson for my audience

....
....
....

Call to action & Hashtags

....
....
....

12th September

Answer another common question
that you get in your line of work

Notes, Ideas, Metaphors, Story

....
....
....

Related lesson for my audience

....
....
....

Call to action & Hashtags

....
....
....

13th September

Ask a true or false question about your topic

Notes, Ideas, Metaphors, Story

....
....
....

Related lesson for my audience

....
....
....

Call to action & Hashtags

....
....
....

14th September

Create a meme based on your industry niche or your audience preferences

Notes, Ideas, Metaphors, Story

....

....

....

Related lesson for my audience

....

....

....

Call to action & Hashtags

....

....

....

15th September

Share a beautiful travel photo

Notes, Ideas, Metaphors, Story

....
....
....

Related lesson for my audience

....
....
....

Call to action & Hashtags

....
....
....

16th September

Show a photo with your current point of view

....
....
....

Related lesson for my audience

....
....
....

Call to action & Hashtags

....
....
....

17th September

Share an image of a famous spot in your city and ask your audience to share a photo of a famous spot from their town or city

Notes, Ideas, Metaphors, Story

....
....
....

Related lesson for my audience

....
....
....

Call to action & Hashtags

....
....
....

18th September

Post a photo of you at work

Notes, Ideas, Metaphors, Story

....

....

....

Related lesson for my audience

....

....

....

Call to action & Hashtags

....

....

....

19th September

Share a post that relates to the current season - and try to tie a thought about how that season relates to your topic. Is there a message in the season that can help inspire or motivate your followers?

Notes, Ideas, Metaphors, Story

....

....

....

Related lesson for my audience

....

....

....

Call to action & Hashtags

....

....

....

20th September

Share a photo or meme that will
make your followers laugh

Notes, Ideas, Metaphors, Story

....
....
....

Related lesson for my audience

....
....
....

Call to action & Hashtags

....
....
....

21st September

Share a post titled 'you know you're a [who your audience are] when….'

Notes, Ideas, Metaphors, Story

....
....
....

Related lesson for my audience

....
....
....

Call to action & Hashtags

....
....
....

22nd September

Create a video, featuring people or products from your business

Notes, Ideas, Metaphors, Story

....
....
....

Related lesson for my audience

....
....
....

Call to action & Hashtags

....
....
....

23rd September

Correct a common misconception
that relates to your industry

Notes, Ideas, Metaphors, Story

....
....
....

Related lesson for my audience

....
....
....

Call to action & Hashtags

....
....
....

24th September

Show off your expertise with a helpful tip

Notes, Ideas, Metaphors, Story

....
....
....

Related lesson for my audience

....
....
....

Call to action & Hashtags

....
....
....

25th September

Post something in celebration
of a company milestone

Notes, Ideas, Metaphors, Story

....
....
....

Related lesson for my audience

....
....
....

Call to action & Hashtags

....
....
....

26th September

Cross-promote your social media channels

Notes, Ideas, Metaphors, Story

....
....
....

Related lesson for my audience

....
....
....

Call to action & Hashtags

....
....
....

27th September

Share an attention-grabbing statistic
related to your industry

Notes, Ideas, Metaphors, Story

....
....
....

Related lesson for my audience

....
....
....

Call to action & Hashtags

....
....
....

28th September

Highlight a customer of the month

....
....
....

Related lesson for my audience

....
....
....

Call to action & Hashtags

....
....
....

29th September

Talk about an event that changed your life

Notes, Ideas, Metaphors, Story

....
....
....

Related lesson for my audience

....
....
....

Call to action & Hashtags

....
....
....

30th September

Search for inspirational quotes related to your topic and share one today - ask your audience to share their favourite quote with you

Notes, Ideas, Metaphors, Story

....

....

....

Related lesson for my audience

....

....

....

Call to action & Hashtags

....

....

....

 OCTOBER

1st October

Challenge your followers to do or implement
something related to your area of expertise

Notes, Ideas, Metaphors, Story

....
....
....

Related lesson for my audience

....
....
....

Call to action & Hashtags

....
....
....

2nd October

Share your products collection or set

....
....
....

Related lesson for my audience

....
....
....

Call to action & Hashtags

....
....
....

3rd October

Post a photo from a recent (or last) event
you attended, and why you think it is
valuable to go to gatherings in person

Notes, Ideas, Metaphors, Story

....
....
....

Related lesson for my audience

....
....
....

Call to action & Hashtags

....
....
....

4th October

Share another platform your
followers can find you on

....
....
....

Related lesson for my audience

....
....
....

Call to action & Hashtags

....
....
....

5th October

Share a list of the upcoming events, challenges, courses, webinars or coaching programs you have coming up in the next 12 months

Notes, Ideas, Metaphors, Story

....
....
....

Related lesson for my audience

....
....
....

Call to action & Hashtags

....
....
....

6th October

Go to YouTube, search for videos on your topic and find the most popular video. Then deliver a livestream with the same title, but in your own unique way and with your own unique content

Notes, Ideas, Metaphors, Story

....
....
....

Related lesson for my audience

....
....
....

Call to action & Hashtags

....
....
....

7th October

Share a post about stress related to your customer avatar and how they can reduce it

Notes, Ideas, Metaphors, Story

....
....
....

Related lesson for my audience

....
....
....

Call to action & Hashtags

....
....
....

8th October

Go to Google News and scroll through the top 20 news articles in your feed. Publish a post that is inspired by one of the articles you found

Notes, Ideas, Metaphors, Story

....

....

....

Related lesson for my audience

....

....

....

Call to action & Hashtags

....

....

....

9th October

Share a video blooper, a fail or something
funny that shows you are not perfect

Notes, Ideas, Metaphors, Story

....
....
....

Related lesson for my audience

....
....
....

Call to action & Hashtags

....
....
....

Create a photo challenge with your audience with a theme, eg: 'jump for joy', 'smile with your pet', 'at my desk' or 'doing exercise' for example

Notes, Ideas, Metaphors, Story

....
....
....

Related lesson for my audience

....
....
....

Call to action & Hashtags

....
....
....

11th October

Snap the point of view of what
you're doing right now

Notes, Ideas, Metaphors, Story

....
....
....

Related lesson for my audience

....
....
....

Call to action & Hashtags

....
....
....

12th October

Share 'A Day In The Life' photo collection

Notes, Ideas, Metaphors, Story

....
....
....

Related lesson for my audience

....
....
....

Call to action & Hashtags

....
....
....

13th October

Think of something completely unremarkable that you did or witnessed today, and share a thought or lesson from it that relates to your avatar. For example, I went to the doctor because i had a sore leg and asked her to amputate it because it was hurting me so much. The doctor told me it was sciatica and all I needed was to sit on a tennis ball, not have an amputation. So I wrote about it and related it to how we can often overreact in business like this too. My audience loved it because it was a real story, but related to them. If you want to read it Google 'Overreacting in Business by Sarah Cordiner'

Notes, Ideas, Metaphors, Story

....
....
....

Related lesson for my audience

....
....
....

Call to action & Hashtags

....
....
....

14th October

Ask your audience to share how they are feeling just using emojis

....
....
....

....
....
....

....
....
....

15th October

Answer another commonly asked
question in your area of expertise

Notes, Ideas, Metaphors, Story

....
....
....

Related lesson for my audience

....
....
....

Call to action & Hashtags

....
....
....

16th October

Share a photo of your set of keys, and talk
about how keys relate to your audience -
a lesson with keys as the metaphor

Notes, Ideas, Metaphors, Story

....

....

....

Related lesson for my audience

....

....

....

Call to action & Hashtags

....

....

....

17th October

Share 3 things that you would stop doing if you won $10million today. Ask your audience to do the same

Notes, Ideas, Metaphors, Story

....
....
....

Related lesson for my audience

....
....
....

Call to action & Hashtags

....
....
....

18th October

Ask your followers about their
favourite teachers or educators

Notes, Ideas, Metaphors, Story

....

....

....

Related lesson for my audience

....

....

....

Call to action & Hashtags

....

....

....

19th October

Share a handwritten message

Notes, Ideas, Metaphors, Story

....
....
....

Related lesson for my audience

....
....
....

Call to action & Hashtags

....
....
....

20th October

Share your Spotify playlist or one of your favourite songs from YouTube. Ask your audience to share theirs too

Notes, Ideas, Metaphors, Story

....
....
....

Related lesson for my audience

....
....
....

Call to action & Hashtags

....
....
....

21st October

Share the view from your office
or room that you work in

Notes, Ideas, Metaphors, Story

....

....

....

Related lesson for my audience

....

....

....

Call to action & Hashtags

....

....

....

22nd October

Talk about a recent (or the last) situation
that inspired you, encouraged you
or motivated you in some way

Notes, Ideas, Metaphors, Story

....

....

....

Related lesson for my audience

....

....

....

Call to action & Hashtags

....

....

....

23rd October

Share something about your local community

Notes, Ideas, Metaphors, Story

....

....

....

Related lesson for my audience

....

....

....

Call to action & Hashtags

....

....

....

24th October

Open up about your greatest fear

Notes, Ideas, Metaphors, Story

....
....
....

Related lesson for my audience

....
....
....

Call to action & Hashtags

....
....
....

25th October

Talk about a hobby you have

Notes, Ideas, Metaphors, Story

....
....
....

Related lesson for my audience

....
....
....

Call to action & Hashtags

....
....
....

26th October

Share a list of fun facts about
yourself or your business

Notes, Ideas, Metaphors, Story

....

....

....

Related lesson for my audience

....

....

....

Call to action & Hashtags

....

....

....

27th October

Pick up a different book to the ones you used in previous posts, turn to page 75 and share a thought, reflection or tip that it inspires for you

Notes, Ideas, Metaphors, Story

....
....
....

Related lesson for my audience

....
....
....

Call to action & Hashtags

....
....
....

28th October

Share teasers for something that you will be doing, running or releasing next month

Notes, Ideas, Metaphors, Story

....
....
....

Related lesson for my audience

....
....
....

Call to action & Hashtags

....
....
....

29th October

Re-share your most popular or
blog post or YouTube video

Notes, Ideas, Metaphors, Story

....
....
....

Related lesson for my audience

....
....
....

Call to action & Hashtags

....
....
....

30th October

Talk about something that you once used
to really struggle with but no longer
do. Share some tips to help others who
may be struggling with that thing

Notes, Ideas, Metaphors, Story

....

....

....

Related lesson for my audience

....

....

....

Call to action & Hashtags

....

....

....

31st October

Post something halloween related, your
thoughts on the celebration and how
it relates to your topic in some way

Notes, Ideas, Metaphors, Story

....

....

....

Related lesson for my audience

....

....

....

Call to action & Hashtags

....

....

....

 NOVEMBER

1st November

Talk about what your days off look like

Notes, Ideas, Metaphors, Story

....
....
....

Related lesson for my audience

....
....
....

Call to action & Hashtags

....
....
....

2nd November

Advertise an affiliate program

Notes, Ideas, Metaphors, Story

Related lesson for my audience

Call to action & Hashtags

3rd November

Introduce the business owners
or members of your team

Notes, Ideas, Metaphors, Story

....
....
....

Related lesson for my audience

....
....
....

Call to action & Hashtags

....
....
....

4th November

Talk about your items' production, manufacturing or execution process - eg 'HOW do you actually make it or 'do' what you do?

Notes, Ideas, Metaphors, Story

....

....

....

Related lesson for my audience

....

....

....

Call to action & Hashtags

....

....

....

5th November

Share how you have overcome the loneliness
and isolation of being a business owner

Notes, Ideas, Metaphors, Story

....

....

....

Related lesson for my audience

....

....

....

Call to action & Hashtags

....

....

....

Share what you thought you'd be when you grew up, and what you actually are now. Ask your audience to share the same!

Notes, Ideas, Metaphors, Story

....
....
....

Related lesson for my audience

....
....
....

Call to action & Hashtags

....
....
....

7th November

Share what's on your computer screen
or what tabs you have open, and why
you are using those sites. Be sure to tag
brands or companies for extra exposure -
they may feature you on their pages.

Notes, Ideas, Metaphors, Story

....
....
....

Related lesson for my audience

....
....
....

Call to action & Hashtags

....
....
....

8th November

Ask your audience a multiple choice
question using the polls feature

Notes, Ideas, Metaphors, Story

....

....

....

Related lesson for my audience

....

....

....

Call to action & Hashtags

....

....

....

9th November

Google 'national and international days' and share about a national 'day' that's happening today

Notes, Ideas, Metaphors, Story

....

....

....

Related lesson for my audience

....

....

....

Call to action & Hashtags

....

....

....

10th November

Choose a different book or eBook to the ones you've picked for previous posts, turn to page 115 and share a post that has a thought, reflection, lesson or tip that is inspired by that page

Notes, Ideas, Metaphors, Story

....

....

....

Related lesson for my audience

....

....

....

Call to action & Hashtags

....

....

....

11th November

National Author's Day – interview an author
or share a book by an author that you love

Notes, Ideas, Metaphors, Story

....
....
....

Related lesson for my audience

....
....
....

Call to action & Hashtags

....
....
....

12th November

Share what you would do if you lost
EVERYTHING and only had 30 days left
to make enough money to survive

Notes, Ideas, Metaphors, Story

....

....

....

Related lesson for my audience

....

....

....

Call to action & Hashtags

....

....

....

13th November

Share a post titled '3 ways that you KNOW you're ready to [what you help people do]'

Notes, Ideas, Metaphors, Story

....
....
....

Related lesson for my audience

....
....
....

Call to action & Hashtags

....
....
....

14th November

Ask about (or share!) life lessons to learn before you're [your age]

Notes, Ideas, Metaphors, Story

....
....
....

Related lesson for my audience

....
....
....

Call to action & Hashtags

....
....
....

15th November

Ask what your followers do to stop wasting their time/procrastinating

Notes, Ideas, Metaphors, Story

....
....
....

Related lesson for my audience

....
....
....

Call to action & Hashtags

....
....
....

16th November

Discuss how to calm down, relax and recharge after a long day doing [your topic]

Notes, Ideas, Metaphors, Story

....
....
....

Related lesson for my audience

....
....
....

Call to action & Hashtags

....
....
....

17th November

Share how you found your purpose in life. Ask your audience what their current life purpose is

Notes, Ideas, Metaphors, Story

....
....
....

Related lesson for my audience

....
....
....

Call to action & Hashtags

....
....
....

18th November

Do a product review - share your views
or feedback about something your
audience might be interested in

Notes, Ideas, Metaphors, Story

....
....
....

Related lesson for my audience

....
....
....

Call to action & Hashtags

....
....
....

Give some tips on how to set realistic
goals in your area of expertise

Notes, Ideas, Metaphors, Story

....

....

....

Related lesson for my audience

....

....

....

Call to action & Hashtags

....

....

....

20th November

Share personal changes you've
made and how you've grown

Notes, Ideas, Metaphors, Story

....

....

....

Related lesson for my audience

....

....

....

Call to action & Hashtags

....

....

....

21st November

Ask for the followers' advice on how
to get more done in less time

Notes, Ideas, Metaphors, Story

....
....
....

Related lesson for my audience

....
....
....

Call to action & Hashtags

....
....
....

22nd November

Feature the tools you're currently using
to keep your business going

Notes, Ideas, Metaphors, Story

....
....
....

Related lesson for my audience

....
....
....

Call to action & Hashtags

....
....
....

23rd November

Share something you love to cook - and then relate how cooking is like [your topic]

....
....
....

....
....
....

....
....
....

24th November

Reveal some habits of famous successful people that relate to your topic

Notes, Ideas, Metaphors, Story

....
....
....

Related lesson for my audience

....
....
....

Call to action & Hashtags

....
....
....

25th November

Share proven tips for staying positive
when doing [what you help people do]

Notes, Ideas, Metaphors, Story

....

....

....

Related lesson for my audience

....

....

....

Call to action & Hashtags

....

....

....

26th November

Share a post related to thanksgiving

....
....
....

....
....
....

....
....
....

Post an image of your Black Friday haul
and/or post your Black Friday Offers

Notes, Ideas, Metaphors, Story

....
....
....

Related lesson for my audience

....
....
....

Call to action & Hashtags

....
....
....

28th November

Share Black Friday specials you're shopping for and/or remind people about your Black Friday Offers

Notes, Ideas, Metaphors, Story

....
....
....

Related lesson for my audience

....
....
....

Call to action & Hashtags

....
....
....

29th November

Share a 'last chance' post about your
Black Friday or Cyber Monday offer

Notes, Ideas, Metaphors, Story

....

....

....

Related lesson for my audience

....

....

....

Call to action & Hashtags

....

....

....

30th November

Show the results of Black Friday

Notes, Ideas, Metaphors, Story

....

....

....

Related lesson for my audience

....

....

....

Call to action & Hashtags

....

....

....

 DECEMBER

1st December

Talk about other entrepreneurs who inspire you or have helped you grow in some way (It's my birthday today, so you could always tag me @ SarahCordiner as my birthday gift! Haha!)

Notes, Ideas, Metaphors, Story

....

....

....

Related lesson for my audience

....

....

....

Call to action & Hashtags

....

....

....

2nd December

Share your proven ways to take control of something in your area of expertise

Notes, Ideas, Metaphors, Story

....
....
....

Related lesson for my audience

....
....
....

Call to action & Hashtags

....
....
....

3rd December

Make a list of alphabetical advice. For example, each letter of your name could be the first letter of a word por sentence that is helpful and inspiring to people

Notes, Ideas, Metaphors, Story

....
....
....

Related lesson for my audience

....
....
....

Call to action & Hashtags

....
....
....

4th December

Write a short autobiography

Notes, Ideas, Metaphors, Story

....
....
....

Related lesson for my audience

....
....
....

Call to action & Hashtags

....
....
....

5th December

Make a list of easy goals to accomplish
before the end of the year

Notes, Ideas, Metaphors, Story

....
....
....

Related lesson for my audience

....
....
....

Call to action & Hashtags

....
....
....

6th December

Share 10 links that you love, that would help your audience

Notes, Ideas, Metaphors, Story

....
....
....

Related lesson for my audience

....
....
....

Call to action & Hashtags

....
....
....

7th December

"Wordless Wednesday': post
pictures without captions!

Notes, Ideas, Metaphors, Story

....

....

....

Related lesson for my audience

....

....

....

Call to action & Hashtags

....

....

....

8th December

Create a pros and cons list related to your niche

Notes, Ideas, Metaphors, Story

....
....
....

Related lesson for my audience

....
....
....

Call to action & Hashtags

....
....
....

9th December

Make a must-have list for your niche that
they could ask to get as gifts for Christmas

Notes, Ideas, Metaphors, Story

....

....

....

Related lesson for my audience

....

....

....

Call to action & Hashtags

....

....

....

10th December

Create a checklist for a specific task or action
related to accomplishing something in your niche

Notes, Ideas, Metaphors, Story

....
....
....

Related lesson for my audience

....
....
....

Call to action & Hashtags

....
....
....

11th December

Share the worst advice you ever
received related to your niche, and ask
your audience to share the same

Notes, Ideas, Metaphors, Story

....
....
....

Related lesson for my audience

....
....
....

Call to action & Hashtags

....
....
....

12th December

Explain how NOT to do something

Notes, Ideas, Metaphors, Story

....

....

....

Related lesson for my audience

....

....

....

Call to action & Hashtags

....

....

....

13th December

Show your most popular blog post this year

Notes, Ideas, Metaphors, Story

....
....
....

Related lesson for my audience

....
....
....

Call to action & Hashtags

....
....
....

14th December

List your favourite things about December

....
....
....

Related lesson for my audience

....
....
....

Call to action & Hashtags

....
....
....

15th December

Share your Christmas offer

Notes, Ideas, Metaphors, Story

....
....
....

Related lesson for my audience

....
....
....

Call to action & Hashtags

....
....
....

Ask your audience what their
favourite experience or memory was
with you this past 12 months

Notes, Ideas, Metaphors, Story

....

....

....

Related lesson for my audience

....

....

....

Call to action & Hashtags

....

....

....

Share tips for buying gifts for people
who are hard to buy for

Notes, Ideas, Metaphors, Story

....

....

....

Related lesson for my audience

....

....

....

Call to action & Hashtags

....

....

....

18th December

Give some tips on how your audience can stay on top of their tasks and goals in your area of expertise over the Christmas season

Notes, Ideas, Metaphors, Story

....
....
....

Related lesson for my audience

....
....
....

Call to action & Hashtags

....
....
....

19th December

Show how you style a Christmas tree

Notes, Ideas, Metaphors, Story

....
....
....

Related lesson for my audience

....
....
....

Call to action & Hashtags

....
....
....

20th December

Share a list of things that you do, review, plan or prepare in December in regards to your business or area of expertise and encourage your audience to do the same

Notes, Ideas, Metaphors, Story

....

....

....

Related lesson for my audience

....

....

....

Call to action & Hashtags

....

....

....

21st December

Share a meditation that you like that
helps you stay calm and centered
during the upcoming busy season

Notes, Ideas, Metaphors, Story

....
....
....

Related lesson for my audience

....
....
....

Call to action & Hashtags

....
....
....

22nd December

Review your most popular product from
this year and how you are planning on
making it even better next year

Notes, Ideas, Metaphors, Story

....

....

....

Related lesson for my audience

....

....

....

Call to action & Hashtags

....

....

....

23rd December

Remind everyone about your
Christmas giveaway!

Notes, Ideas, Metaphors, Story

....
....
....

Related lesson for my audience

....
....
....

Call to action & Hashtags

....
....
....

24th December

Share a 'peek into your private life' video or photo of your Christmas set-up at home, your family, partner or how you are spending your Christmas

Notes, Ideas, Metaphors, Story

....

....

....

Related lesson for my audience

....

....

....

Call to action & Hashtags

....

....

....

25th December

Christmas – make a post about this holiday

Notes, Ideas, Metaphors, Story

....

....

....

Related lesson for my audience

....

....

....

Call to action & Hashtags

....

....

....

26th December

Boxing Day – create a post about the gifts you've received and given

Notes, Ideas, Metaphors, Story

....
....
....

Related lesson for my audience

....
....
....

Call to action & Hashtags

....
....
....

27th December

Share a reminder post about what exciting things customers can look forward to from you next year

Notes, Ideas, Metaphors, Story

....
....
....

Related lesson for my audience

....
....
....

Call to action & Hashtags

....
....
....

28th December

Write about the top 10 things
you learned this year

Notes, Ideas, Metaphors, Story

....
....
....

Related lesson for my audience

....
....
....

Call to action & Hashtags

....
....
....

29th December

Share a 'before and after' post regarding your own growth this year. For example, how many clients you had in january compared to now, how many students, sales, followers, subscribers etc that can use to show your growth and inspire others to follow you into the new year to grow too

Notes, Ideas, Metaphors, Story

Related lesson for my audience

Call to action & Hashtags

30th December

Share your New Year's plans and resolutions
and ask the followers to share theirs too

Notes, Ideas, Metaphors, Story

....

....

....

Related lesson for my audience

....

....

....

Call to action & Hashtags

....

....

....

31st December

Share what 'word' or 'theme' you will be going into the new year with, and ask your audience what theirs is too

Notes, Ideas, Metaphors, Story

....
....
....

Related lesson for my audience

....
....
....

Call to action & Hashtags

....
....
....

SUMMARY

I hope that you have found these prompts useful to inspire new ideas and new ways to think about your content creation and community engagement.

I would love for you to join my Facebook group *'**Entrepreneur To Edupreneur - Course Creators, Coaches & Consultants'*** and let me know how you found these prompts - if they've helped your engagement and following grow!

If you'd like ot take your business to the next level and REALLY see your leads, sales and reputation grow, then come and join my 'Edupreneur Academy' where I will walk you through the journey of online business success: www.sarahcordiner.com/academy

If you have any questions or feedback, feel free to email me on sarah@sarahcordiner.com

In the meantime, I wish you great success!

Sarah Cordiner

www.sarahcordiner.com/academy

Made in the USA
Monee, IL
14 August 2023

40993637R00230